" Be Happy "

Color Me Yellow

by Fred Sergeant

This book is dedicated to Nat, Daisy, Cody, and Odie. All of whom have taught me lessons and brought meaning to my life.

WHY YELLOW?

I Love Yellow!

For many years, I have been synonymous with the color Yellow. To be honest, I am an attention hound for sure and I'm sure my selection of this color as my favorite had at least something to do with that. I was the middle child!

Yellow has represented wisdom and intellect throughout history. It has represented happiness, clarity, and sunlight. It is a favorite color in advertising because it stands out among all the colors.

Yellow is a Primary color, one of 3 colors that can't be produced by mixing other colors together. It's a cheerful, happy color that exists on its own.

I have loved its positive nature so much that I make it a personal challenge to find everything I can in yellow. I always have a yellow car, watch, shoes, you name it. Nicknamed "Yellow Man" by some, my bank office always had lots of yellow, including the clock on the wall. Customers would say, if the day was dark and gloomy, all they needed to do was walk into my office.

Color Me Yellow means color me happy. And happy is what we all strive for…

1

I was born and raised in Gainesville, Florida on April 1, 1969, no fooling.

We were a middle-class family; both of my parents worked. My father worked at the local Ford dealership in the parts department and was very well known in town. He had no formal education and was often angry and unhappy about his thankless job. He had extremely low self-esteem. He came home nightly, smoked a pipe or cigarettes, and downed Budweiser like it was water. This was his escape and any distraction from this routine could send him into a rage.

My mother was a manager at a local dentist office. She didn't have any formal education either and was insecure about her body. She would worry constantly about money but loved the nicer things in life. Designer purses, Chanel No. 5 perfume, you name it. She dreamed of living the rich, high society life and managed to find a way to dabble in that lifestyle by buying things on sale at department stores like Maas Brothers.

My family was rounded out by my older half-brother, Richard (from my mother's first marriage), my younger brother Brian, and my grandmother (my mother's mother) that I called "Nana."

Richard was the introverted, artistic type. Five years my senior, he mostly stayed in his room and collected comic books as a hobby.

Brian is a year and nine months my junior. He was a saver! He used to surprise us all with the stack of cash he managed to put away from saving his allowance. He showed an interest in the stock market at a young age and even had one of the first personal computers.

Then there was me, Freddie, the middle child. Quiet and shy, I loved to sing and spent my money as soon as I got it. I always had trouble sleeping from nightmares.

What a group we were, right?

GOOD IDEA #1

To find your inner joy, begin by being GRATEFUL for what you already have.

2

As a child, I remember dreaming about being an adult. I would fantasize about driving my own car and having my own place. I guess some would say I was an old soul? Maybe I just wanted to escape from the prison I felt like I was living in.

We were literally locked in our room from the outside at times. Beat with the belt until we had stripes on us. Even threatened with a gun, and had our heads held in a pillow until I thought I might suffocate.

How I didn't turn out to be a crazy person or jail bird I don't know.

It was a chaotic house, my nerves were bad, and I had little power to do anything about it.

I was a good kid. Sure, my younger brother and I would fight sometimes, but more times than not, I was quiet, did well in school, and didn't cause my parents any trouble.

From a young age, I was always fascinated by Halloween. It was a chance to escape from reality. A day you can be anything. It is a day to have fun and be whoever you want to be. I even liked it better than Christmas and I still do to this day.

Growing up, I always dreamed of being a famous singer. It was an outlet for me. I would save my allowance to buy Anne Murray records; I just loved her voice and I would study and mimic her tone as I sang along. My parents liked country music and Anne was somewhere between country and pop. She was the artist I really connected to.

I just knew if I was famous, I could leave that place.

I was good in school, but that definitely didn't mean I liked it. Since I was always a chronic insomniac, I was tired all the time and it made school a real drag. I couldn't stand memorizing facts and taking tests. All I really wanted was to be in the real world...

2nd Grade

GOOD IDEA #2

You can't always control what happens to you in life, but YOU CAN control how you react to it.

3

At age 10, a stray dog wandered into our yard.

Mother was a neat freak and Dad was busy drinking, but to my surprise, we were allowed to keep him. We named him Tramp. He was a mutt. We believed he was part pit-bull and part Rhodesian ridgeback.

In any case, Tramp was my first experience with a dog. I remember how attached I got to him. He brought excitement and a sense of innocence to the household.

Tramp had some funny habits! So many times, he would pull up the stake he was tied to and take off running. I can remember chasing him down the road dragging the long chain behind him. Thinking about it now, I guess we were lucky he never got hit by a car.

One thing I'll never forget about Tramp is how much he hated it when we went to school. Would you believe that silly dog figured out that we needed our backpacks to go to school, and if we forgot and tossed them on the couch, you could count on him to be standing there guarding them. As you reached to grab it, he showed his teeth and growled. I always imagined he was telling us, "you are not going anywhere!"

He wasn't always easy to fool, but sometimes we would trick him by ringing the doorbell or bribing him with a treat. I sensed his love and innocence; it brought something special to my life.

He was a family member from the start. Even Mom and Dad really loved him too.

Good ole Tramp.

GOOD IDEA #3

Really look into the eyes of a dog. Observe and feel the love they exude. Appreciate the joy they find in the smallest things.

Their purity is something to behold. It can teach us to connect to that part of our own spirit.

I don't think it is a coincidence that God spelled backwards is Dog.

4

For us kids of the 70s, learning to be independent was something that came at an early age. At my house, we cleaned the house from top to bottom for a weekly allowance of $5.00. We dusted, vacuumed, cleaned bathrooms, cooked dinner, did dishes, and even rubbed our parents' feet with lotion after a long day at work.

It's funny to see the look on their faces when I talk to parents. They look at me like I have three heads when I tell them I made the family dinner as young as age 10 or 11. My brother and I also did laundry and mowed the lawn. Contributing to the household and respect for your parents was expected back then.

I know the new generation, for the most part, doesn't seem to have their kids do these things. I'm thankful we did; it taught us how to care for ourselves and gave us a better work ethic than what is displayed nowadays.

But it wasn't all work growing up, I remember riding bikes the most. There was a freedom in taking off on a bike and riding the neighborhood. It seemed so safe back then, we never really had to worry about anything except an occasional bully. Mother would blow a whistle when it was time to come home… you'd better believe we'd hurry back or there was hell to pay!

On Saturdays, we would ride to a local 7-11 and grab some candy and gum, while picking up a newspaper for our parents. The excitement of that ride was amazing! Our backyard was a wonderland where we would pretend to be super heroes or chase our dog Tramp around.

Some weekends, our Nana would take us to Uncle Bob's house to swim in his pool. Afterwards, we would have an ice cream from a local place called Doug's Dairy Twirl or burgers at In an Out Hamburgers or we'd go to the Second Chance bakery/bread store for honey buns or donuts.

I remember those bright summer days - our parents were working their antique business and without those trips to the pool and the ice cream place, it would have been pretty boring. Nana was a hoot, she'd show us old westerns and feed us beanie weenies and French fries…those memories are strong, a sweeter, simpler time.

GOOD IDEA #4

Spend time with loved ones every chance you get. We all grow up and have our own lives, but you will never regret time spent with family.

5

My mother died from breast cancer on October 28, 1983. She was 38. I was standing over her at 1:40pm when she took her last breath.

I remember not knowing how to feel.

I didn't cry.

It's still so strange to me, but I didn't cry.

Maybe I was in shock? Maybe I feared what our dad might do now that she was gone? Or maybe I just had unresolved feelings that left me confused...

I do know that I felt very alone. My brother had more in common with my father and I knew it was going to be me against them. But I was ready. I had an independent nature that would not be denied, and I always felt that I needed to be myself, no matter what other people thought.

At 17, and just shy of my high school graduation, I moved in with my Nana. Once I left my childhood home, I rarely returned. I never spent another night in that house. That chapter of my life was over and there were so many left to be written that simply didn't include that environment.

Melissa was such an important part of my life back then. To this day, she's one of the sweetest people I've ever known. We had been together for a few years at this point and she was such a good girlfriend.

We both worked, me at Publix as a bag boy and her at Western Sizzlin' stocking the salad bar, but those were just jobs. Melissa put in so much time helping me – emotionally, financially, and even with school. I had a hard time sleeping and it caused me to miss a lot of school, but she would visit me at Nana's with notes from class so I wouldn't fall behind.

Melissa's family was also good to me. They fed me dinners and always made me feel like I was welcome. They were there for me at a time I needed a family.

GOOD IDEA #5

Following trends is overrated. If people are wearing white shirts and everyone is doing it to fit in or not be criticized for being different, but you want to, say wear a yellow shirt, then DO IT! Who cares what the neighbors think? The older you get, the less you care what people think, *trust me*.

6

While working at Publix supermarket, I got a job tip from a friend. It would take my life in a new direction. She told me a bank named "The Big E" was hiring tellers and starting them at over $5/hour! I was only making about $3.85/hour at the time and this sounded like a gamechanger.

I went home and told Nana and she sprang into action! She suggested we go to Belk's department store and buy a suit so I could go interview for the job. It was a grey suit that paired wonderfully with my famous clip on tie that I ended up wearing for quite a while. It was the beginning of a career that would span more than 25 years (but we'll circle back to that later).

Melissa and I lasted a few more years. We graduated at the top of our class; she was #4 and I was close behind at #6. We went to senior prom and even got to go on a trip to St Augustine together. I loved Melissa and everything about her. She was sweet and giving and I was so lucky to have her as my girlfriend, but I was hiding a deep secret…

I knew I was attracted to men.

During my relationship with Melissa, I wouldn't kiss her or have any physical interaction beyond holding hands. I knew she was cute, but my attraction and desires laid elsewhere. I often wondered how she put up with me for so long. She was such a sensitive young lady that believed you should wait until marriage to be more intimate, so she never pressured me into anything.

Melissa was my first of many heartbreaks. A little more than a year after graduation, I wrote her a letter and told her what I thought was going on with me. I was scared to death to tell her and the whole thing was very painful for both of us.

I wanted to try counseling, but her friends told her to forget it, they knew it wouldn't work. As the reality set in, we couldn't even bare to see each other for a long time, but that wasn't the end of our story.

I didn't know it at the time, but like I said before, this was only the beginning of many heartbreaks in my life.

GOOD IDEA #6

A single interaction can take your life in a direction you never imagined. Be alert to all that is around you and stay positive. Just when you think you know where you're going, it can all change in wonderful ways. It may not make sense to you until later, so run with it.

7

I was a 21-year-old single gay man and I was afraid of being alone. I was so unsure what the future had in store. This was a time when people didn't talk about being gay. There were even secret meetings for gay men and women. These meetings were social events but were also for support. Telling my brother, Nana, and my Dad was ahead and I feared the reactions.

Nana had a hard time with it at first. She even talked to her doctor, who said I could "go either way." I already knew I couldn't. My dad was always such a macho guy with the naked women calendars and everything, so I was expecting the worst, but he and my brother took it well - what a relief. Now, my hope was that I could meet someone to share my life with.

I spent more than a year secretly writing letters to a professor. We would send weekly letters, so I purchased a PO Box, that way no one would know. Some letters were about advice and questions I had. Some letters were sexual fantasies that I wrote involving him or a fictional guy. The relationship never got physical, but he helped me tremendously and ended up introducing me to a student group where I met other gay people my age. I really wanted to meet someone to date.

That year, I went to my first gay club, with my dad of all people! I was so scared, but he really helped by being there. All I really wanted was a male version of Melissa, but I would discover that was a tall order.

GOOD IDEA #7

To be FREE, you have to be who you are. You have to release your fear and face it head on. It will strengthen you and move your journey forward.

8

For the next few years I would go to the nightclubs in search of Mr. Right. Instead, I often found Mr. Right for the night. I always ended up settling - I figured it was better than nothing. I'd get attached to someone and have my heart broken. It was a pattern that repeated for years.

I met a group of friends and ended up moving into a townhouse in the southwest part of Gainesville. We hung out together regularly and even had special nights during the week, everyone loved our famous *Melrose Place* nights. I took great comfort in what had become my new family. It was that time I met my good friend Scotty and my first love…

Joe.

Joe was a guy I would have never thought to date. He was into pot, pain pills, and just liked to hang out and "rest." I, on the other hand, had never tried pot and was interested in traveling and staying busy all the time. I am a hyper, let's go go go, kind of guy. We were mismatched from the start, but I fell in love with this man because of his sweet nature and cute smile.

Joe was a self-proclaimed bisexual; I should have known heartbreak was right around the corner, but I dove in like I always did, throwing caution to the wind. For the next three years, we would live together and remain almost secret lovers. He hadn't come out to his parents and never had any intention of discussing it with them. He often warned me not to get too attached, some day he was going to marry a woman and that would be that. It was already too late though, I loved him. I shed so many tears over the years as I struggled with this relationship, hoping he would change his mind.

After graduating from Art School at the University of Florida, Joe left and moved to Tampa. That was it, he was gone.

It was a low point in my life - I even considered killing myself. I was just so tired of all the hurt.

Soon after, though, a single word changed everything...

Cancer.

A fight for my life would take me in a new direction.

GOOD IDEA #8:

If your happiness is dependent on someone else, you will always be disappointed. You must find the happiness that resides inside of you. Only then can you share that happiness with someone else, instead of putting the pressure on them to supply it to you.

9

In May of 1993, I was having a health issue that went beyond the heartbreak Joe left me with. The left side of my neck was growing larger and I didn't know why. At the time I had a cat named Max and my doctor thought I might have cat scratch fever. He also suspected I could have HIV.

After testing negative for these, I went through different antibiotics for the next couple months with no success. It looked like a baseball was growing out of the side of my neck!

Over the Fourth of July weekend, I went to the emergency room throwing up buckets of black bile from my intestines. A biopsy was ordered immediately.

I woke up alone in the hospital room the next day with a doctor at my bedside. My worst fears were confirmed. He began to explain that I had a rare cancer called Burkett's lymphoma and that I might only have 2 months to live without aggressive chemotherapy.

Two months…

My survival instinct kicked in immediately. Death wasn't an option.

I started thinking about the travelling I had done over the previous few years. I wasn't making much money at the time, but I saved and went on a trip to England and then the following year I took a trip to Egypt. These trips awakened a part of me that wanted to see more of the world, something my mother never got to do.

I needed to survive! I had too many places I wanted to see.

I jumped into my treatment. I was ready to fight and stay positive along the way. My hospital room had pictures of Paris on the wall - that was my next travel goal and I wouldn't make it there if I was gone. It was like a "vision board." I used pictures of my goals as something to drive me and keep me on track.

The road ahead would be tough but unexpected angels would be sent to my aid.

GOOD IDEA #9:

If you believe it, you can make it happen. It's more than positive thinking, you must envision it's already done. It can't hurt and it's a positive way to live.

10

During my treatment, I experienced pain I never thought I could handle. High fevers, sharp pains, mouth sores, extremely painful bowel movements – it was agony. My hair, something I was always so concerned about, was gone; I didn't even have eyebrows or eyelashes for goodness sake!

My Nana set up a hospital bed in the living room of her house. That's where I stayed for many months, when I wasn't in the hospital. I was in the hospital so many times I lost count, often as many as ten days at a time. I remember they wouldn't discharge me until my temperature was normal, so I tried to fool the nurses by drinking ice water right before they came in the room. It never worked. I hated it there, the environment was so *cold* and I longed to be home.

Nana would come to my hospital room every day and bring me scrambled eggs, bacon, and toast. She was already in her 70s but would sit with me all day and not leave until late afternoon or early evening. Looking back, this still amazes me.

At the hospital, there was a young guy named Rick who took me to X-ray one day. Rick would become an angel who looked after me. He even spent the night in my room after working there all day and put cold rags on my head. Later, he spent nights at Nana's house when I was home. I was a stranger to him! Do you feel that? I still get chills thinking about his kindness.

A young lady named Chris would also come and pray for me at the hospital. She and I both worked for the same bank but didn't know one another. She brought food and kept me positive. I still have the bible she gave me with a special dedicated verse. She was another angel that blessed my life at such a trying time. She told me that I was placed in her mind by God one day, so there she was - wow.

My doctor, Dr. Montoya, was another blessing. He was smart and had the best bedside manner you could ask for. He took the time to write a letter to the Moffitt Cancer Center in Tampa to get me into their new bone marrow unit. It was an amazing facility.

GOOD IDEA #10:

No matter your circumstances, surround yourself with positive people. Laugh, eat your favorite meals, and keep yourself active. A positive state of mind can aid in healing the body more than any medicine on Earth.

11

The bone marrow unit was quite an experience. For more than 40 days, I was confined to a room that I couldn't leave. There was an entire wall that was purifying my air and I wasn't allowed to even take a shower! I had to take sponge baths with bottles of purified water each day.

I remember entertaining the nurses with my boom box, playing 80s music like Boy George and Madonna, classics that I still love.

I was the youngest person in the whole unit.

When you're hyper it can be a real problem being confined. I was going crazy; I watched way too much TV and couldn't even read a book without constantly checking how many pages were left in the chapter. One day they finally figured out how to get some of that excess energy out - they brought a treadmill into my room!

I often sat at the window thinking about what was going on in the outside world. The holidays zoomed by and before I knew it Thanksgiving and Christmas had passed and we were into the New Year. It didn't matter though, I only had one goal, get this done so I could move on with my life.

And I did. I beat it.

After leaving the unit, I started to rebuild my strength and return to my job at Barnett Bank. I was anxious to prove I hadn't lost a step. Wouldn't you know it, I went right back to winning the sales awards and recognition I had built my banking reputation on prior to my leave of absence. I didn't know it at the time, but my banking career was about to take off and I would double my income in less than two years.

In a leap of faith, I would leave this company of 11 years to try a new one.

After years of doing well and winning awards, I was tired of being passed over. I felt I would never get the job I deserved at Barnett Bank. The good old boys controlled the company and no matter how well I did, I was not going to be considered for a higher role. Not that Fred guy. The *gay* guy.

Julie, one of the managers at Barnett, was leaving to go to another bank, so I decided to ask her if she would consider letting me go with her. She had reservations. She knew I was a good employee, but she wondered if I could be an assistant manager. Of course I could and I assured her as much!

She brought me along and six months later I landed my own branch manager job in Orlando.

There I was, starting to make a name for myself again.

In my 20s after going through cancer treatment.

GOOD IDEA #11:

Fear is in the mind. You must look beyond the mind to your deeper core to overcome it. Not doing so will keep you imprisoned and unable to achieve your highest potential and dreams.

12

Who knew there was so much pressure and stress associated with being a branch manager! I always knew I would be good to my employees, but I also knew I would push myself to be number one. I worked hard and went out cold calling on businesses in Orlando to build a name for my branch. I had contests and incentives for my employees to drive production. In the end, we won Branch of the Year and I won Branch Manager of the Year in my first year!

In my personal life, I was in my first relationship since having cancer. It was a very up and down situation. In the beginning, I was ready to make it work no matter what. I moved to Deltona, where he had a house, and I got to experience canine love again. He had a dog and loving her reminded me how much I missed having a dog.

In the beginning, things were going well. We even had a marriage ceremony at an Orlando church. It wasn't legal, but we wanted to make a point. On my side, only my cousin Judy and her husband Sam attended. My close friends, who had become family, were also there. They saw things early on I wasn't willing to see.

My partner had a bad temper and an inner rage. It never got physical, but there was a lot of emotional stress. I wasn't perfect either, of course. We all bring "luggage" into a relationship. But, I refused to accept failure and stuck with the union for more than four years. I was afraid of being alone again, but one day, I just knew I had to overcome that fear. We talked and decided it was best we parted ways.

Later we would reconnect as friends and are to this day. We both changed and moved on in life.

Before we split up something magical happened…

Daisy.

She was named after my mother's favorite flower. I didn't know it at the time, but that little girl beagle would become the dog of my lifetime. Daisy would see me through so many moves and life events…but more on her later.

I found out my good friend Scotty had started looking for a place to live in Orlando, so I made plans to move in with him. I needed to get away from Deltona and start over. I was still addicted to relationships though, so I started going out in Gainesville on weekends. I met someone new almost right away and after seven short months, I was ready to move back to Gainesville. My friends could only shake their heads in disbelief.

GOOD IDEA #12:

Patterns of behavior can be broken if you face them head on and decide you want to change. Look in the mirror and talk to yourself. You might have the best advice of all.

13

Daisy and I returned to Gainesville and I moved in with my new partner. He was working on his PhD in microbiology; he was smart, from South America, and had such a sexy accent! We moved into a small apartment, close to where I use to hang out with my old gang on the southwest side of town.

He had a three-year-old daughter who came and stayed with us some in the summer. He had remained friendly with his ex-wife and they made arrangements for him to spend time with her. As far as she was concerned, I was "just a friend" or "roommate," of course.

She was too young to understand; I was ok with that. He wasn't out at work either, but that changed as the years went on. Eventually, I would socialize with him and his coworkers.

In December of 2001, my dad became ill. He came out of a coma just long enough to make peace with me and other family members before taking a turn for the worse. My brother Brian was living with him at the time and they were very close. He passed away at the age of 56. It's crazy how short life can be and how quickly things can change.

When my partner found out he needed to move to Knoxville, TN for his job, I thought a move might be good for us. We were 5 years into the relationship, with signs it was not working out, but like I always did, I tried to hold on. So, I resigned from my job and prepared to move to Tennessee.

Before the move, Daisy got a brother. We adopted a boy beagle and named him Cody. He was an innocent and skittish boy. Daisy was less than 2 years old at the time.

Was I really moving to Tennessee? I went kicking and screaming, but off the 4 of us went to a new state to start a new life.

GOOD IDEA #13:

Listen to that voice in your head. Maybe it's intuition, maybe it's a spirit looking over you and whispering in your ear.

14

After arriving in Tennessee, I got a new job as a bank manager in downtown Knoxville and my partner started settling into his job. He was working at a national lab with people from all over the world. He was loving the move, but I was often tearful and sad that I left Florida and my friends behind. I was working with the general public and going to manager meetings, but no one wanted to sit next to the guy from Florida.

I began to plan international trips each year to keep me distracted. I hadn't been on one in many years and decided to ask Brian if he wanted to go. Over the next five years, we traveled to Brazil, Australia, Japan, Greece and Hawaii. Ok, so Hawaii isn't international, but it was far enough and exotic enough that it felt like it was! They were incredible trips with so many funny stories of the Sergeant Brothers on the move.

I also made a lot of trips back to Gainesville just for the weekend to see Nana and Brian. Ten hours of driving each way, just to escape. I remember how excited I would be to see the "WELCOME TO FLORIDA" sign and how sad the drive back to Tennessee was.

My partner's job was only supposed to be for three years, but he decided he wanted to stay.

Things weren't right between us, though. We started experimenting with introducing a third guy into our sex life. There was an intimacy that was missing in our lives and I thought at least it wouldn't be a secret and it wouldn't be cheating. It seemed like a good idea; we had rules for safety and how it would all go down. In the end, it was disastrous to an already troubled union.

We didn't have the same spiritual beliefs or the same feelings for Daisy and Cody. We were so different and fought all the time.

When counseling didn't help, we split. I immediately set my mind to finding a job in Florida. Even though Tennessee wasn't for me, I met some incredible people that I love very much.

After a couple of job offers, I decided on Flagler Beach. It just felt right to me. Daisy, Cody, and I headed off into the unknown.

GOOD IDEA #14:

Don't let anyone or anything stop you from reaching your goals or pursuing your passion. If you want to travel, then travel. If you feel like your dog is your kid and the people around you don't understand that, surround yourself with people who do.

15

December 20, 2008, I remember my friends driving away from my new condo in Flagler Beach. I was 39, alone, and in an unfamiliar place. I was hired over the phone and hadn't even met my boss yet. I knew this was a new beginning, and though it seemed scary, I was ready to move forward. I knew I was in the right place. Flagler Beach is beautiful and peaceful, and I always dreamed of living by the ocean.

I jumped into my bank manager job right away and was fortunate to have a great staff. They were very welcoming and we became quick friends. We took the branch performance to new heights of excellence, while laughing and cutting up along the way. We always had a blast together, from Sasha doing exercises in the lobby, to Anna and I singing in the drive thru. Looking back, I treasure that time so much.

Two months into my new life, I decided to go on the computer to meet someone. I wasn't sure if I would meet someone serious or just have some fun. Who am I kidding? Of course, I was looking for something serious! Hello, serial relationship addict here!

And I did. I found the love of my life – my soulmate.

I was ten years his senior, but he would teach this old dog some new tricks. From eating healthy, to spiritual growth, I became a better person because of him.

More importantly, he loved the kids! Especially Cody, with whom he instantly had a special bond.

His name is Nat. A name he gave himself after moving to the US from India. We met at a movie theatre in Daytona Beach, and I remember he was dressed so well I thought he was a playboy and for some reason, I was underdressed that day in shorts and a t-shirt – it makes me chuckle thinking about it today!

We went to see the movie "MILK," starring Sean Penn. He put his head on my shoulder during the movie and it felt so great. It felt right. He came back to my place after the movie and met Daisy and Cody for the first time. I knew there was something special about this guy.

Nat lived with his family, about an hour from me, and we decided we would see each other the following weekend. We have been together ever since, a decade as I write this.

For the first 7 months, we only saw each other on the weekends. He would come over Friday night and stay until Sunday night. I quickly became attached, and after just two months, I told him I loved him outside of a restaurant in Flagler Beach.

His response, "Thank you." As the kids say, "awkward!"

Nat explained he had thrown the "L" word around too easily before and just wasn't ready for that at this stage in our relationship. I remember sleepless nights, which are not uncommon for me, where I would go for a walk while he slept. I was fretting over why he hadn't told me he loved me, too.

I decided to go to counseling and take advantage of some sessions I had available through the bank. I felt I had always messed things up with relationships in the past and wanted some advice on how to do things right this time. I went for a few months, until I felt I had a better handle on things.

And then, after 9 months of dating (2 of which we lived together), Nat looked me in the face and told me he loved me. He said he might have known for a little while but wanted to be sure.

It was official.

We were a couple and I was enjoying the best time of my life.

GOOD IDEA #15:

If you never take chances and always play it safe, you risk going nowhere…and that, is the greatest risk of all.

16

Nat and I started really getting to know each other at our condo in Flagler Beach. I met his friends Jessica and Colette and we all became great friends. We grew so close, we started feeling like siblings! We spent almost every weekend together. No outing was complete without our close friend Ariann. We would go to art shows, concerts, you name it. So many road trips to St Augustine!

Shortly after Nat moved in, we adopted a precious third kid, Odie. We saw him at Petsmart on a Saturday and struggled with the decision of getting a third pup. Ultimately, we gave in and brought him into the family. Odie is a Chihuahua-Italian Greyhound mix, with a personality bigger than life.

It's was during this period, that Nat and I planned our first of many **EPIC HALLOWEEN PARTIES**! That's right, <u>underlined</u>, CAPPED, and **bolded**, they were that epic!

The annual party took on a life of its own and often involved months of planning and preparation. Being the Halloween junky that I am, it was always a blast.

Nat and I also took our first trip together, a vacation to San Francisco. For the next five years, we would travel to different cities in California. We visited San Francisco (twice), Los Angeles, Santa Barbara, Santa Rosa, and San Diego. By this time, I had left the bank and started working as a manager of not one, but two branches of a credit union in Palm Coast.

Five years in, Nat's family really wanted him to live closer to them. They lived on the river in South Daytona and we were a good 45 minutes away. Nat and I started looking at houses in Daytona and within a short time, we were buying a beachside house in Daytona Beach Shores.

I was sad to leave Flagler Beach and our friends that lived nearby. It was a change that would take some adjustment, but I knew we could drive over any time we wanted.

In October 2014, we made the move to Daytona Beach Shores. The condo was behind us and a new adventure began. We found a great home, with a second level overlooking the river and just a five-minute walk to the beach. Plus, there was the added bonus of the kids having a yard to play in for the first time in their lives!

GOOD IDEA #16:

Laugh a lot – especially at yourself, it's very therapeutic.

17

Our house is great for entertaining! The upstairs bar was famous for parties throughout the decades. If only those walls could talk!

One bedroom became the kid's room. We used it when company came over and we needed to keep them safe. This room, also known as the "80s room," is decorated with albums and framed prints from the 1980s.

Meanwhile, Nat was hard at work on the front and back yards. He did a lot of landscaping and started a garden of fresh herbs and vegetables. A tree stump in the corner of our back yard was turned into a beautiful Buddha temple. The place was starting to feel like home.

Daisy was 15 at this time and struggling with the stairs. We decided to block the stairwell for her protection. Odie was still able to go around the back of the stairs and crawl up if he wanted to. He was the only one small enough to do it.

Cody and Daisy had free reign of the backyard. Cody would charge the fence at the neighbor's cat and roar like a lion! Daisy would just wander around and check things out. Wild Odie was kept on a leash, as the side fences are low enough he could jump right over them.

At the time, I was driving from Daytona Beach Shores to Palm Coast every day for work. Little did I know, more change was coming soon.

GOOD IDEA #17:

When you feel like something is missing, take a look around you and be grateful for the things you do have. Part of us always wants more. Take a pause and think about what you already have!

18

I had been in banking for 26 years, mostly serving as a branch manager. I was good at it, and almost always exceeded my goals. I give a lot of credit to my teams, as you can't achieve these things on your own. I always did my best to make them feel appreciated, and we had fun while accomplishing our objectives.

But I was getting burned out on banking.

After work, I secretly started studying real estate, part of the plan for a new chapter in my life. I wanted to leave, but I was afraid of the unknown and banking had given me a decent living.

I also considered starting a pet sitting business. I had done some of this in my 20s and loved being around dogs and cats. The idea was born to combine pet sitting and real estate and start my own business.

After dealing with some "politics" at my current work place, including a supervisor who was unethical, I decided it was time for me to leave banking and take that leap of faith again. I resigned in August of 2014 and agreed to work a notice until January 30, 2015.

During my 5-month notice, I continued to work just as hard at achieving my goals. It's just part of me to compete and push myself to be the best, (maybe there was also the added incentive of getting my annual bonus in January, but that was just gravy). After coming in second many times, the branch won BRANCH OF THE MONTH in November of 2014. We were so proud; the branch hadn't received this recognition in many years. Then, the most incredible thing happened, BRANCH OF THE YEAR 2014! We had done something the Palm Coast West Branch had never done. I was leaving at the top of my game and this would be my legacy.

Starting February 2015, I was on my own. I owe thanks to a supportive partner that allowed me to take this "jump" into the unknown.

I began to book and promote pet sitting and make my way into the real estate market. I passed the real estate exam my on first attempt! I would soon discover it was not as easy as it looks. Not only is there lots of competition, but there are expenses and financial challenges you can't imagine. Let's just say, if you decide on real estate as a career, have at least a year of bills put aside before you start.

Making about half my old salary, year one was mind blowing. But I was free, and boy was I happy!

Fred the Realtor

GOOD IDEA #18:

If reinventing yourself was easy, everyone would do it.
If you want a different life – just jump into it!

19

As I headed into my second year of being an entrepreneur, I had high hopes of ramping up my business. The first year taught me some tough lessons, and I was excited to see what 2016 would bring.

In January, Nat and I noticed something was not right with Cody. He did not have an appetite, and we thought he might just be going through a "picky" phase. He was still eating treats and seemed to be active.

A week later, Cody decided he was not interested in treats, and we decided to have him evaluated. We took him to an animal hospital in Ormond Beach, and the doctor took an x-ray of his abdomen.

As the doctor walked back from the x-ray machine, I could feel my nerves on end. What would he tell us about our precious boy? He said it wasn't good, there were masses around the liver area. I remember being in shock. We thought we would leave with an antibiotic, and he would be fine. My heart sunk.

We decided to take Cody to an animal hospital in Flagler Beach for a second opinion. The doctor told us it was time. She said he had internal bleeding and was eaten up with cancer. I couldn't believe what was happening. He was charging the fence a couple weeks before, and there we were planning our goodbyes.

We decided we could not let our baby suffer. He was refusing water now and would hold his face less than an inch from the water bowl and not drink. On a Saturday, from the parking lot of the animal hospital, I made a call to a vet that comes to your home. Monday morning would be the time.

That Sunday night, Nat and I slept with Cody on the floor of our living room. One on each side of him. Nat had a beautiful dream, confirming we were doing the right thing. He awoke with Cody staring at him and his paw on his shoulder. Cody had imparted the message.

Cody went peacefully that Monday morning, with both of us loving him. My heart was broken, and surely would never be the same. Almost 14 years old, our son, had moved on from his earth life with us. Our love for him remains as strong as ever.

GOOD IDEA #19:

When you are worried about the future or thinking about the past – pause a moment. Think about the *Now*, the present moment. What is happening around you? Are you missing it by being on auto-pilot? This moment can't be brought back.

20

CODY

This part of the book is dedicated to Cody and some things I want you to know about him. He was certainly special enough to warrant a section of his own.

From the moment I met Cody, I knew he was a rare soul. He had a sweet nature that was hard to put into words. His original name was Angel, I changed it to Cody. Truth is, he was, and still is, an angel.

Cody was a perfect canine kid. He did his business when you told him to, ate his food without any problems, and was always ready to play and give love. He could just sit on the couch and look at you from across the room, and you would have to smile at his handsome face.

Cody was always so innocent. Anything out of the ordinary, worried him. If you put a cardboard box in the middle of the floor, he would be afraid of it.

During thunderstorms, we tried everything to comfort him to no avail. You would likely find him in the shower or hiding somewhere. At night, especially during summer storms, he would try to climb on my face. I would hold him under the covers to make him feel safe, but it rarely worked. We would take his bed to the bathroom so he could rest.

His favorite thing was playing with sticks. He would jump like crazy and go nuts catching and running to retrieve them. For him, it was better than any toy you could buy.

His relationship with Nat was special. I teased Nat about stealing my boy, but I loved their bond. I would often find them cuddled together in bed or on the couch, and I would say, "What the hell is going on here?"

Nat would normally say something like, "Don't disturb our love."

Cody knew how to hug. I would get down on the floor and he would put a paw on each shoulder and give me a kiss. Some of the best kisses of my life. I remember cuddling with him on the couch, and I used to think in my head, "This is what touching heaven feels like."

I am not just saying it because he was our son, but Cody was just so handsome! He always looked like a model, with perfect facial features. If you ask me, that dog should have been in calendars!

Cody taught me so many things. He taught me to roar like a lion, even if you are scared inside. He taught me to enjoy simple things, like a stick on the ground. He taught me that you don't need words to show your love. And maybe most importantly, he taught me there is still pure love in the world.

I will miss you Cody, until my last breath. I will talk to your spirit every day, until the day comes when we see each other on the other side.

I love you!

GOOD IDEA #20:

Hug your kids often, whether they be two-legged or four-legged. Close your eyes and think about this incredible gift you have been given.

21

I never saw it coming, but 2016, would be a turning point in my real estate career. I teamed up with a friend at the company, Becky, and we took the market by storm. We had multiple listings with amazing success! Each of us brought different strengths to the team, we called ourselves the SUNSHINE STATE TEAM – "The Sunny side of Real Estate." We do business the old-fashioned way, with hard work and honesty. Clients can call or text us at 9pm on a Sunday night, and get immediate responses. We hold other agents accountable and make our clients' interests a top priority.

The year would end with less income than my bank job still, but better than the year before. That was a positive sign. I was now confident in what I was doing.

I got a new car in 2016, too! My trademark YELLOW auto would now be a 2014 Fiat 500L Trekking that I named Joy. The name was fitting for the car and for the new life I was now experiencing. The freedom of being in control of my own daily life… priceless.

GOOD IDEA #21:

If you are a visual person like me, cut out pictures and place them on a "vision board." It's a fun and exciting way to set goals.

22

2017 opened with a celebration I will ALWAYS cherish, DAISY'S 17th Birthday! Our girl was honored with a party, complete with a beautiful daisy cake made by our chef friend, Rosie. One room was filled with large pictures of her throughout the years, and attendees wrote her messages. She received gifts, everyone told their favorite Daisy stories, and we showered her with love.

Daisy had been an important part of my life for many years. Stubborn as a mule, but we loved her all the same. Her health had started declining recently and she was experiencing mini seizures or some type of neuropathy. She would suddenly start jerking and her eyes would flicker. The condition seemed to come and go; she rolled with the punches like a strong girl.

Business was going well for Becky and me as we continued to close deals and get new listings. I was loving the real estate life, despite the fact that some elements are out of your control. You can't make a house appraise or a loan officer approve a loan. The uncertain income had Nat and I discussing "supplemental" options.

At the end of May, I got a call about Becky. I remember it well. She was at the hospital and they thought she was having a stroke. My heart dropped, she's more than just a business partner, she's my friend. Long story short, Becky was diagnosed with a non-cancerous brain tumor, and underwent surgery for its removal. She is doing well now and taking recovery day by day. We ended the year selling more than 2.5 million dollars in real estate with 16 transactions. We were a tough couple of survivors!

As the year drew to a close, Nat found out about a class that could be taken to become a certified nurse assistant. Though it didn't pay much, it would at least offer a consistent income. I took the one-week crash course in November and started my self-study for the state exam. I was out of my comfort zone, but I was going for it.

Daisy's symptoms continued to mount, and we noticed she was drinking lots of water. Blood tests revealed she was living with 25% kidney function. We tried special foods and supplements, but we knew her time was limited. We took her to the beach and started giving her foods she loved, like browned hamburger and gravy. Nat prepared blended sweet potatoes to give her some fluids and needed nutrition. She even enjoyed the gingerbread I made for the holiday season; sometimes that was all she would eat.

Our sweet Daisy was letting us know to prepare, but how could I prepare for her departure? She was too much of my heart. Nat stood crying in the kitchen one day looking at her. He said he had never seen someone so strong.

We made it through the holidays, with 2018 ahead.

GOOD IDEA #22:

Celebrate milestones with your loved ones. Your time is more valuable than any gift.

23

As the clock struck midnight, I kissed Daisy to bring in 2018. Our girl was just a week from her 18th Birthday, but I wasn't sure she would make it.

January 8th arrived, Daisy had made it to her 18th Birthday! We celebrated with neighbors and friends and "Miss America" was the center of attention again. She had willed herself to make it, like she knew I needed it.

On January 11, 2018, just three days after her 18th Birthday, Daisy let us know it was time. Her body was failing, and we couldn't let her suffer. A daughter for nearly two decades, was leaving this world for a better one. My heart, in many ways, will never be the same.

After Daisy's passing, the tributes began to mount: a bench in the front yard, metal art in the backyard, a tattoo on the right shoulder, and many more little reminders. Our friend Colette did an amazing pen and ink of her for the living room. Our friend Terri had done one of Cody a couple years before. The King was once again with his Queen. Daisy and Cody were together - Angels to look over us.

I focused on my CNA state exam and figuring out how to add some additional income for the year. By the end of January, I had passed the state exam! I was excited, but also overwhelmed with emotion. I know Nana and my sweet kids were with me that day. I cried as I walked to my car with the happy news. A new chapter was beginning for me, all part of my continued REINVENTION.

I went to Granny Nannies and looked into using my CNA license part-time so I could continue to sell real estate. Within a week I was blessed with an 88-year-old client that needed my help. I continue to work for this family and consider it a true gift.

GOOD IDEA #23:

When you lose someone you love, remember that the body is always meant to be temporary. The soul, or spirit energy, is eternal.

24

DAISY

This part of the book is dedicated to Daisy and some things that make her so special.

Where do I start with Daisy?

She was an independent, stubborn ball of love, from the moment she could only fit in the palm of my hand, all the way to the end.

It's like she knew when I needed to get to work; more times than I can count, I found myself waiting for her to do her business. She would never go when I needed her to, only when she felt like it!

On one occasion, I was living in an apartment complex and I was walking her early in the morning. I must have said, "Daisy do your business!" a hundred times. I was getting more and more concerned about getting to work on time. Suddenly, this lady walks to her open window and says, "Daisy, please do your business!" I was so embarrassed, but that was Daisy.

Daisy was very independent. I would like to cuddle with her, and she would to some degree, but then she would pull away and go lay down by herself.

She never needed much affection. I would often grab her, and kiss her, while saying, "Love me bitch!"

After that, you could count on her throwing her head back and belting out that famous beagle howl. Such a diva!

She was vocal if she wanted something. While the boys would silently stare a hole through you for food, Daisy would let you know what she wanted. No silent approach for this girl! There were many times Nat and I almost got kicked out of hotels from her sharing her displeasure.

Daisy, however stubborn, was a sweet natured dog. She never growled at another dog or human being her entire 18 years of life. She could be trusted with anyone or anything. I can even remember a cat coming up to her and rubbing its face against hers.

For years, Daisy was a therapy dog. I would take her to a senior retirement center and let her lay in bed with the residents to cheer them up. They would beg me to make her howl. All it would take was for me to say, "Squirrel Daisy, a squirrel! "She would look up into the trees and go to town on her howling. The residents loved it and laughed out loud every time.

As she got older, she got stronger. Even after losing her hearing and most of her vision, she was the picture of strength and beauty. Most people couldn't believe how old she was. They thought she was a puppy, even at 15. Hence, her "Miss America" nickname.

Daisy too, taught many lessons. It's ok to be independent. Speak up for what you want in life. Be gentle and kind to everyone and everything. You can be young at any age. No matter what your circumstances, you can find the strength to push through.

Daisy was amazing! One in a million. My daughter forever, even now in spirit form.

GOOD IDEA #24:

When it seems like you can't keep moving....keep going anyway! Power through, even though you might think it's impossible – you can!

25

ODIE

This part of the book is all about Odie.

At the writing of this book, Odie is 13 years old and has been with our family for 8 years. Odie was 5 years old, when we got him from Second Chance Rescue in Palm Coast, Florida.

From what we know, Odie had been returned to the Orlando Humane Society many times. He had been put on the list to be euthanized. Second Chance Rescue took him in and experienced a couple of returns themselves.

Odie was accepted by Daisy and Cody from the start. He was also great with us. But we soon learned Odie had some quirks. For one, he does not like kids...any kids. Maybe he was abused by a child early in his life, we don't know.

Odie would also have occasional "accidents" in the house, no matter how many times we walked him. We found a solution, training him to use puppy pads in the bathroom.

Odie can also be aggressive with certain people. If he sensed an odd energy, let's just say, they didn't forget meeting him!

As the years have passed, Odie has mellowed quite a bit. He seems to have realized we are never giving him away, and that he is in a loving home for the rest of his life. He is very affectionate and loved by all that meet him. He has a personality that fills a room and is so loving you would wonder how anyone could have given him up.

I'm glad they did.

We have witnessed Odie bounce 3 feet in the air like a kangaroo. We have seen him show his teeth, in typical Chihuahua fashion, when Nat gets him fired up. He has made us laugh and smile since the day he entered our home.

We won the LOVE LOTTERY I often say. My favorite thing to say to Odie is, "You're little…and I like it! You're cute…and I Like it! And cute and little go good together!" He just looks at me like I am crazy, maybe I am, but I love him so much!

Odie's lessons have been great ones as well. Never think you won't be loved, there are always people who will. Be quirky, the people that love you will appreciate your uniqueness. You can find love late in life. Sometimes, the best thing for you is waiting just down the road. Cut loose and be wild sometimes.

Odie is our only child right now. He is the center of our universe, as he deserves to be.

Sergeant   81

GOOD IDEA #25:

Rescue a dog or cat. The reward is PRICELESS!

26

NANA

I feel the best way to express my thoughts about her is through a poem I wrote. She was always there for me. She often had a negative outlook, but I understood her. She internalized her pain and never let it go. From childhood memories of taking us places on weekends, to bringing me breakfast every day at the hospital during my cancer, she was there.

> The warmth of the sun's
> rays shine brightly
> through the open
> window A welcome sight
> as it illuminates the room
> filled with painful
> memories
>
> Your love of family gives
> you strength even in
> your darkest hour Your
> place in history secure as
> the rock that was always
> there

A lifetime of holidays
dance in the minds of all
your loved ones Your
strength and
determination always on
display A given you'd
always be the center of
the show

You learned to enjoy the
simplest of pleasures A
colorful bird, the taste of
something sweet, a car
ride on a summer day A
lesson for all of us that
remain

This human life comes
with lessons A contrast
between positive and
negative spectrums But
your lasting mark will be
one of loyalty and
dependability Your
unwavering LOVE
always shining through

Dedicated to Myrtle
Caswell (Nana) by Fred
Sergeant (10/4/2017)

Birthday Celebration after cancer with Nana (left).

GOOD IDEA #26:

Put the past in your rear-view mirror. Holding on to anger corrodes the container it is held in.

27

NAT

My soulmate.

At the writing of this book, we have been together for 10 years, married 6.

Nat has continued to teach me many things about health, and life in general. I listen to more than he thinks I do, but I have some hard habits to break, like all of us.

I have anxiety sometimes. Nat is calm and cool as a cucumber, most of the time. He has given me tips on how to relax and quiet the mind and he has taught me that love is through actions, not words.

No one has ever understood me as deeply. He also shares the love for our babies at a level no one else has.

Nat gives and cares for others, without wanting any personal recognition. In fact, he hides from the spotlight. He is the most non-materialistic person I have ever known, and never really buys anything for himself.

I have often said, "He could live under a tree, on a mountain, and be happy."

From serious talks about life, to cooking me healthy meals, to helping me start a new career and chase my dreams, encouraging exercise, the love he shows me through his actions are blessings from above.

GOOD IDEA #27:

Have a partner, spouse, or friends who help you grow.

MORE GOOD IDEAS

In the following 22 pages, there is what I consider a GOOD IDEA on each page.

Why 22? I don't know yet, but that is the number my spirit guides keep sending to me.

One day, it will make sense I am sure. I think each idea, standing alone, like they do earlier in the book, ensures they are contemplated a little deeper.

I hope some of these speak to you.

GOOD IDEA #28:

Go on trips. You might regret purchases, but never experiences.

GOOD IDEA #29:

Eat healthy, but have one or two cheat meals a week if you want. Enjoy what you love in moderation.

GOOD IDEA #30:

Write down your "bucket list." See it so you can work on it.

GOOD IDEA #31:

IF you can have a pet, get one. Their innocence and love are positive energy you want to have around you. They make you smile and laugh daily.

GOOD IDEA #32:

Do some level of exercise every day. Keep moving now, so you still can later.

GOOD IDEA #33:

Volunteer for a cause that has meaning for you. You will cherish this time.

GOOD IDEA #34:

Take walks alone in nature. On the beach, your favorite park, anywhere. Listen and pay attention to all that is around you. It's a form of meditation.

GOOD IDEA #35:

Always BELIEVE you can win. Always BELIEVE you can handle any challenge.

GOOD IDEA #36:

Talk to yourself. In the mirror or not, these can be the best pep talks.

GOOD IDEA #37:

Have a GRATITUDE journal. The more you see what you are grateful for the more you will receive in your life.

GOOD IDEA #38:

Drink more water. Yes, we have all heard this, but we don't do it. Water is so good for every organ, including the skin!

GOOD IDEA #39:

Try new things. Maybe buy a canvas and some paints and see what you create.

GOOD IDEA #40:

Surround yourself with your favorite color. It's your personality on display. Be happy.

GOOD IDEA #41:

Work hard for what you want. The harder you work the luckier you will be.

GOOD IDEA #42:

Continue to learn. Read about subjects that call to you.

GOOD IDEA #43:

Start a collection. It doesn't have to be something expensive. It's like a treasure hunt.

GOOD IDEA #44:

Take care of yourself first. Don't care what other people think.

GOOD IDEA #45:

Don't settle for the wrong relationship. Learn to be happy alone. Maybe the right person is meant to come at age 40, 50, or beyond.

GOOD IDEA #46:

Take pictures of happy events. They will make you smile for years to come.

GOOD IDEA #47:

When you are alone, listen to music you love and sing to your heart's content. Sometimes a voice, a lyric, or the music itself touches your soul.

GOOD IDEA #48:

Read a positive message or saying to begin each day. It starts you off in the right direction.

GOOD IDEA #49:

Don't compete or compare yourself to others. Your journey is unique.

25-year Cancer Survivor

FINAL WORDS

In my 50 years on this planet, I have grown up in a stressful household, learned to accept my sexuality, lost loved ones at an early age, defeated cancer, dealt with heartache, and lived with chronic dizziness from Meniere's disease, to name a few.

I have been blessed with loving babies, great friends, good jobs, continued health, a soulmate, a great house, and so many other things.

I have reinvented myself, after 26 years of banking, and acquired state licenses in real estate and healthcare. I have had a pet sitting business, done paintings, sung on stage, and written books and poetry. I have been blessed to have taken trips around the world and have stepped foot on 6 of the 7 continents.

What lies ahead for Fred Sergeant? I am not sure, but it will involve challenging myself, and living as positive a life as this "Yellow Man" can.

I hope this book inspires the courage in you to challenge yourself and be the best you can be!

Sergeant 115

CPSIA information can be obtained
at www.ICGtesting.com
Printed in the USA
BVHW030919210719
553998BV00001B/165/P

9 780999 058138